Dr. Lori-ellen Pisani's

Practice

The Art and Architecture of Teaching

The Alignment Series: How Human Systems Learn
Volume 2 of 3

By Lori-ellen Pisani, PHD

Copyright

Dr. Lori-ellen Pisani's - Practice

Global Copyright & Licensing Notice

Restricted Use – License Required

The following uses are prohibited without a signed licensing agreement executed by BuildingBlocs Literacy LLC:

- Classroom, school, district, or organizational instruction
- Professional development, training, or coaching delivery
- Facilitated group use, workshops, or seminars
- LMS, digital platform, or online course integration
- Reproduction or distribution of exercises, tools, or assessments
- Use in nonprofit, religious, corporate, clinical, or government settings

Purchase of this book does **not** grant instructional, training, facilitation, or institutional use rights.

Protected Components (Non-Public Use)

The following components are proprietary and may not be reused, shared, adapted, or implemented without an executed license:

- PKP™ instructional structure, sequencing, and methodology
- Educator reflection tools, assessment items, and exercises
- Facilitator guides, training materials, and pacing frameworks
- Downloadable resources, printable tools, or derivative materials
- Narrative voice, coaching posture, and instructional design logic
- Digital, video, audio, or AI-assisted instructional extensions

Unauthorized Use Prohibited

No portion of this system may be:

- Facilitated in educational, training, counseling, or professional settings
- Uploaded to or shared through digital platforms or LMS systems
- Repackaged, resold, sublicensed, or rebranded
- Used to create derivative instructional or training products

These restrictions apply across all U.S. states and territories, tribal jurisdictions, and all international jurisdictions recognized under the Berne Convention.

For Licensing, Training, or Official Use

BuildingBlocs Literacy LLC
Attn: Dr. Lori Pisani

info@**BuildingBlocs**.org
www.**BuildingBlocs-**Academy.com
www.BuildingBlocs.org

For Licensing, Training, or Official Use

BuildingBlocs Literacy LLC
Attn: Dr. Lori Pisani

info@**BuildingBlocs**.org
www.**BuildingBlocs-**Academy.com

Dedication

For educators who continue to teach with integrity
even when systems make it harder than it should be.

Lori-ellen Pisani, PHD

Table of Contents

Introduction

Chapter 1 Foundations of Daily Practice

Posture as Instructional Decision-Making

Chapter 2 Reading Readiness in the Room

Recognizing Cognitive and Emotional Readiness Without Lowering Rigor

Chapter 3 Facilitating Awareness Through Instruction

Attention, Noticing, and the Language That Makes Thinking Visible

- Using Academic Tasks to Surface Thought
- Awareness Before Comprehension
- Attention as an Instructional Outcome
- Picture Walks, Book Talks, and the Architecture of Awareness
- Language as a Tool for Orienting Thought
- Classroom Illustration: Awareness in Practice
- Awareness Is Not a Separate Skill

Chapter 4 Regulation as Instructional Support

Pausing, Scaffolding, and Task Design Inside the Lesson

- What Regulation Looks Like When Learning Is Possible
- Regulation Is Visible Before It Is Named
- Regulation as Readiness, Not Compliance
- Instruction Can Restore Regulation
- Classroom Illustration: Regulation Inside Instruction
- Scaffolding as a Regulatory Tool
- Pausing as an Instructional Move
- Why Regulation Does Not Require Emotional Naming
- Why This Matters

Chapter 5 Literacy as the Primary Carrier

Reading, Writing, Speaking, and Listening as Practice Spaces

- Discussion and Text as Neutral Ground
- The Four Domains as Instructional Containers
- Why Stories Carry More Than Information
- Text as Neutral Ground
- Classroom Illustration: Literacy Holding Complexity
- Speaking and Listening as Paired Practices
- Writing as Thinking Made Visible
- Why Literacy Protects Rigor

Chapter 6 Designing Tasks That Invite Thinking

Ambiguity, Choice, and Productive Struggle

- Why Over-Clarity Can Shut Learning Down
- The Misunderstanding of Clarity
- Ambiguity as an Instructional Necessity

Chapter 10 Practice With Boundaries

What Facilitation Is, and What It Is Not

- Preventing Drift Into Compliance or Therapy
- Why Boundaries Matter in Instruction
- Facilitation Defined
- What Facilitation Is Not
- Classroom Illustration: Boundaries in Action
- Preventing Drift Into Compliance
- Preventing Drift Into Therapy
- Why Boundaries Protect Everyone

Afterword

What Remains
What This Book Leaves Behind
A Note on Professional Trust
Where This Work Lives
Final Word

Introduction

Why This Book Exists

This book begins from a simple instructional truth:
practice is where instruction either holds or breaks.

Educators are not short on knowledge. They are not short on strategies. What they are navigating, every day, is the gap between knowing what should work and responding when it doesn't.

Classrooms do not unfold in controlled conditions. They move. Students shift in readiness. Attention fragments. Tasks land unevenly. Even well-designed lessons begin to strain under real conditions.

This is not failure.
This is instruction.

The problem is not that teachers lack skill. It is that practice is often discussed as if it were stable, predictable, and repeatable. It is not.

The purpose of this book is not to introduce new methods.
It is to clarify what is happening **inside instruction as it unfolds**.

Groundwork established that learning depends on conditions that precede content.
This book addresses what happens next:

what educators do when those conditions are present, unstable, or breaking in real time.

This is not a book about adding more.
It is a book about working **inside what already exists, moment by moment, decision by decision.**

What This Book Is About

This book examines **instruction in motion**.

It focuses on how educators:

- read the room while teaching

- adjust pacing without lowering rigor

- design and modify tasks as students engage with them

- use questioning to extend thinking rather than close it

- respond to error without shutting down participation

- support decision-making as part of learning

- maintain boundaries while remaining responsive

This is not a collection of strategies.
It is a study of **instructional decision-making under real conditions**.

At the center of this work is posture, not as a concept, but as something enacted continuously through:

- pacing

- language

- response

- restraint

- adjustment

The goal is not control.
The goal is **coherence while teaching is actually happening**.

This Book Within a Three-Book Series

This volume is the second in *The Alignment Series: How Human Systems Learn*, authored by Dr. Lori-Ellen Pisani and developed within the Pisani–Kershaw Program (PKP).

Each book serves a distinct purpose while building on the others.

Book One: Groundwork

The structure that allows good teaching to breathe

Groundwork defines the instructional conditions that support learning:

- awareness

- regulation

- interaction

- reasoning

It clarifies what must be present before instruction can function consistently.

Question answered:
What must be true in a classroom for learning to occur?

Book Two: Practice

How instruction holds, shifts, and responds in real time

This book moves from conditions into action.

It examines how instruction operates when:

- readiness is uneven

- pacing breaks

- engagement fluctuates

- lessons begin to derail

Focus:

- reading readiness and pacing

- task design that invites thinking

- questioning and feedback during instruction

- decision-making as a visible outcome

Question answered:
What does teaching look like when it is actually happening?

Book Three: Alignment

Protecting instructional coherence at scale

The final book examines systems:

- leadership

- curriculum design

- policy and implementation

It focuses on how instruction is supported or disrupted across classrooms.

Question answered:
How do systems sustain good instruction without reducing it to compliance?

CASEL Cross-Section Alignment

This book aligns fully with the **Collaborative for Academic, Social, and Emotional Learning (CASEL)** framework while intentionally resisting checklist-based or skill-isolated interpretations.

Rather than treating CASEL competencies as discrete targets, *Groundwork* addresses them as **integrated capacities embedded within instruction**.

CASEL Domain	How It Is Addressed in This Book
Self-Awareness	Emerges through noticing within tasks
Self-Management	is supported through pacing and structure
Social Awareness	Develops through shared academic work
Relationship Skills	Practiced through interaction and discussion
Responsible Decision-Making	Becomes visible through choices made during learning

This alignment ensures national SEL coherence **without converting instruction into SEL delivery**.

ELA Alignment

Literacy remains the primary instructional carrier.

Reading, writing, speaking, and listening function as **the spaces where thinking becomes visible**:

- Reading supports interpretation and inference

- Writing organizes and refines thought

- Speaking tests reasoning publicly

- Listening engages perspective and evidence

Literacy provides structure without requiring personal exposure, allowing students to engage with complexity safely and rigorously.

How This Book Connects to the Broader Series

Practice operates within the PKP instructional system:

- *aligned with Groundwork principles*

- *connected to educator tools and guides*

- *integrated with student-facing materials*

- *supported by leadership and implementation structures*

It serves as the **operational layer***, where foundational ideas become instructional action.*

How to Read This Book

This book is not meant to be skimmed for strategies.

Its value lies in how its ideas connect across moments of instruction.

Each chapter examines a different aspect of practice, but together they form a single argument:

instruction succeeds when educators can respond in real time without losing purpose.

Nothing more is required.

Practice

An Introduction to the Pisani–Kershaw Program (PKP)

The **Pisani–Kershaw Human Development & Life Readiness Program** is a comprehensive, skills-based educational framework designed to support learning readiness, emotional regulation, reasoning, and decision-making across developmental stages.

PKP is not a curriculum in the traditional sense.
It is instructional infrastructure.

The program exists to address a reality educators recognize immediately: students cannot consistently access academic learning unless foundational conditions, emotional readiness, regulation, safety, and relational trust, are present. Rather than treating these conditions as separate initiatives or behavioral add-ons, PKP embeds them directly within instruction.

This approach allows schools to support the *human prerequisites for learning* without diluting academic rigor or overstepping professional boundaries.

What PKP Is Designed to Do

The Pisani–Kershaw Program equips educators with a coherent framework for:

- Supporting **learning readiness** before content demand

- Strengthening **self-regulation** and attentional capacity

- Making **thinking and reasoning visible** within academic tasks

- Aligning social, emotional, and cognitive development with instruction

- Preserving educator authority while avoiding compliance-driven practices

Importantly, PKP does not ask educators to become therapists, counselors, or behavioral technicians. It affirms teachers as instructional professionals working inside complex human systems.

How PKP Is Structured

PKP is built as a **modular system**, allowing institutions to adopt components independently or as a fully integrated framework.

Core Developmental Capacities Addressed

- Awareness and attention

- Regulation and readiness

- Communication and interaction

- Decision-making and consequence reasoning

- Accountability and repair

These capacities are not taught as abstract concepts. They are developed through **task design, language, pacing, and facilitation** within academic instruction.

Chapter 1

Groundwork of Daily Practice

Posture as Instructional Decision-Making

Why Consistency Matters More Than Strategy

Instructional practice is frequently framed as a matter of strategy selection. Professional discourse emphasizes methods, routines, and evidence-based techniques, often implying that instructional effectiveness emerges from the correct assembly of tools. While strategy matters, this framing obscures a more foundational reality: **teaching unfolds under conditions that cannot be standardized.**

Classrooms are not stable environments. They are human systems shaped by developmental variability, emotional fluctuation, relational dynamics, and contextual disruption.

Students arrive with uneven readiness. Attention shifts. Cognitive load accumulates. External factors intrude without warning. Even the most carefully planned lesson can destabilize within minutes.

These conditions do not represent failure. They represent the ordinary context of instruction.

In *Groundwork*, teaching was established as a human act before it is a technical one (see *Groundwork v3*, pp. 21–23). This chapter extends that premise into daily practice by examining what allows instruction to remain coherent when strategies alone are insufficient. The central claim is this: **instruction is stabilized not by consistency of strategy, but by consistency of posture**. Strategies must change. Posture cannot.

What the Field Commonly Gets Wrong About Practice

A persistent misunderstanding in educational discourse is the belief that effective practice minimizes variability. Under this assumption, successful instruction is characterized by smooth delivery, uninterrupted pacing, and visible compliance. Variability, whether cognitive, emotional, or behavioral, is framed as disruption to be managed or corrected.

This assumption is deeply embedded in accountability-driven systems. Teachers are often evaluated on their ability to maintain order and fidelity, reinforcing the idea that deviations from plan represent weakness rather than responsiveness.

This interpretation is incorrect.

Variability is not a problem to be solved. It is a condition to be navigated. Attempts to eliminate variability through rigid control frequently reduce access to learning, particularly for students whose readiness does not align with imposed pacing or structure.

Groundwork reframed observable behavior as instructional information rather than interruption (pp. 24–25). That reframing is essential here. Daily practice does not succeed by suppressing variability, but by responding to it without abandoning instructional purpose.

Instruction Happens Inside Human Systems

No classroom operates in isolation. Instruction occurs within nested systems: individual students, peer groups, classroom norms, school cultures, and broader institutional pressures. Each layer introduces variables that shape engagement and readiness.

Students bring with them:

- developmental differences

- emotional states

- relational histories

- external stressors

Teachers bring:

- professional judgment

- instructional intent

- institutional constraints

These systems interact continuously. Planning can anticipate some variables, but not all. Effective instruction therefore requires a stabilizing orientation that does not depend on ideal conditions.

That stabilizing orientation is posture.

Posture as a Professional Orientation

Posture refers to the educator's stable orientation toward learning, behavior, and decision-making. It is not a technique, nor is it synonymous with classroom management. Posture governs how teachers interpret classroom information and determine responses under uncertainty.

Posture shapes:

- whether disengagement is treated as defiance or data

- whether confusion prompts correction or recalibration

- whether disruption triggers control or assessment

Strategies are situational. They change with class composition, time of day, emotional climate, content demands, and external pressures. Posture is not situational. It remains constant even as strategies shift.

As established in *Groundwork* (pp. 26–27), educators exercise professional judgment continuously, often without explicit deliberation. Posture anchors that judgment. When posture is stable, strategy changes are intentional. When posture erodes, strategy changes become reactive.

Consistency Reconsidered

Consistency is commonly equated with procedural repetition. Under this interpretation, consistency requires doing the same thing in the same way regardless of context. This view misunderstands both development and instruction.

Effective consistency resides in **predictability of response**, not uniformity of method.

Students quickly discern whether a teacher's responses are grounded in observation and reasoning or driven by urgency and control. When educators consistently pause, assess conditions, and adjust instruction while preserving purpose, students experience stability even as methods change.

This stability supports engagement. It does not dilute rigor. Rigor depends on sustained access to thinking, not uninterrupted pacing.

A Necessary Counterargument: Rigor and Accountability

Concerns are often raised that responsiveness undermines rigor, particularly in accountability-driven systems. From this perspective, slowing pace or adjusting delivery is viewed as lowering expectations or compromising standards.

These concerns are understandable. However, they conflate **rigor with speed** and **standards with compliance**.

Adjusting pace does not simplify content. It creates space for students to process complexity. Preserving rigor requires maintaining cognitive demand, not enforcing uniform timing. As *Groundwork* notes, access to learning is a prerequisite for meaningful assessment (pp. 28–29).

Posture allows educators to maintain high expectations without insisting on identical pathways. It supports rigor by sustaining engagement rather than prioritizing coverage.

When Lessons Derail

Lessons derail. Attention shifts. Emotional responses surface. Confusion interrupts momentum. These moments are not exceptional; they are inherent to teaching within human systems.

In compliance-oriented models, such moments are treated as failures requiring correction. The response is typically procedural: redirect behavior, restate expectations, increase control. While these responses may restore order, they often narrow access to learning.

Posture-driven instruction responds differently. Disruption is interpreted as instructional data. The educator assesses:

- cognitive load

- emotional readiness

- task design

- pacing

Adjustments are made to delivery rather than intent. Instruction continues, recalibrated rather than abandoned.

This reflects the stance articulated in *Groundwork*: response, not reaction, sustains learning (pp. 28–29).

Classroom Illustration: Grade 3 Literacy Instruction

A teacher begins a shared reading lesson aligned with curricular goals and prior instruction. The objective is clear. The text is familiar.

Within minutes, engagement becomes uneven. Several students whisper. One student looks away from the text. Another displays physical tension, raised shoulders, clenched pencil.

The teacher does not correct behavior. She does not restart the lesson. She adjusts pacing.

She states neutrally:
"Let's slow this down. I'm seeing different reactions, and that tells me something about how this is landing."

She rereads the passage aloud, modeling phrasing. She asks:
"What part was unclear just now?"

One student identifies a word. Another remains silent. The teacher addresses the word briefly and continues.

The instructional objective remains intact. The method shifts. No escalation occurs.

This response reflects posture. Behavior is treated as information, and instruction proceeds without loss of purpose.

Why This Matters for Professional Practice

Teachers are frequently placed in systems that reward visible control over instructional responsiveness. In such contexts, posture erodes under pressure, and strategy becomes a substitute for judgment.

This chapter argues for the opposite orientation. Teachers must be supported, professionally and structurally, in responding rather than reacting. Posture provides that support by anchoring decision-making in observation, interpretation, and intent.

When posture is consistent:

- instruction remains coherent under pressure

- students experience stability without rigidity

- learning continues despite disruption

This does not make teaching easier. It makes it aligned with how learning actually occurs.

This Chapter's Contribution

The contribution of this chapter is the articulation of **posture as the stabilizing mechanism of daily instructional practice**. While *Groundwork* established posture as an ethical and relational stance, this chapter locates posture within moment-to-moment decision-making.

Posture is not abstract. It is enacted every time instruction encounters uncertainty.

Chapter Knowledge Check

1. In this chapter, instructional posture is best understood as:

    - A. A classroom management technique

    - B. A set of consistent instructional routines

    - C. An educator's stable orientation toward decision-making

    - D. A response to behavioral disruption

2. Why does the chapter argue that consistency matters more than strategy?

    - A. Strategies are unnecessary in effective classrooms

    - B. Strategies cannot address variability

    - C. Strategies change, but posture stabilizes instruction

    - D. Consistency reduces planning demands

3. In the classroom illustration, the teacher demonstrates posture by:

    - A. Correcting disengaged students

- o B. Restarting the lesson

- o C. Treating behavior as instructional information

- o D. Lowering expectations

Chapter Close

This chapter establishes posture as the foundation of daily practice. The chapters that follow examine how this posture shapes instructional decisions related to readiness, awareness, regulation, literacy, questioning, feedback, and decision-making.

Posture does not remove complexity.
It allows educators to work within it, intentionally.

Chapter 2

Reading Readiness in the Room

Recognizing Cognitive and Emotional Readiness Without Lowering Rigor

Pace as an Instructional Decision

One of the most persistent instructional tensions educators face is the relationship between **pace and rigor**. In professional discourse, pace is often discussed as a logistical concern, how much content can be covered within a given time frame. Rigor, by contrast, is treated as a measure of cognitive demand, frequently conflated with difficulty, volume, or speed.

This chapter challenges that separation.

Pace is not a neutral delivery variable. It is an instructional decision that directly shapes students' access to thinking. When pace is misaligned with readiness, either too fast or too slow, students disengage. When disengagement occurs, rigor is not preserved through insistence; it is lost through inaccessibility.

In *Groundwork*, readiness was defined not as a fixed student trait, but as a **moment-to-moment condition shaped by context, task design, and relational safety** (see *Groundwork v3*, pp. 41–45). This chapter builds on that foundation by examining how educators read readiness in real time and adjust pace without collapsing expectations.

The Myth of a "Right Pace"

A common instructional error is the search for an optimal pace, a tempo that, once established, should be maintained across lessons and learners. This belief is reinforced by pacing guides, scripted curricula, and time-bound assessments that imply learning unfolds uniformly.

It does not.

Readiness fluctuates within a single lesson, often minute by minute. Cognitive demand accumulates. Emotional states shift. Environmental factors intrude. A pace that was productive at the start of a lesson may become inaccessible moments later, not because the content has changed, but because the learners have.

Importantly, this fluctuation is not evidence of poor planning. It is evidence of instruction occurring within human systems.

Teachers who cling to predetermined pacing in the face of visible disengagement often do so out of fear, fear of falling behind, fear of appearing ineffective, fear of deviating from expectation. The result is instruction that continues in form but not in function.

Readiness as an Observable Instructional Condition

Readiness is frequently mischaracterized as internal and therefore unknowable. While readiness does involve internal processes, it is also **observable through interaction with instruction**.

Indicators of readiness include:

- sustained or fragmented attention

- physical posture and orientation

- response latency

- engagement with task language

- tolerance for ambiguity

These indicators are not diagnostic tools. They are instructional signals. In *Groundwork*, behavior was reframed as communication rather than compliance data (pp. 24–25). Readiness operates within that same frame. Students continuously communicate whether instruction is landing, overwhelming, or failing to engage.

The task of the educator is not to correct these signals, but to interpret them.

Pace as a Gatekeeper of Access

Pace determines whether students can remain cognitively present long enough to engage with complexity. When pace is too fast, students disengage through confusion, avoidance, or frustration. When pace is too slow, students disengage through boredom, inattention, or behavioral drift.

Both conditions reduce access to rigor.

This is a critical distinction: **rigor does not increase when pace accelerates beyond readiness**. Nor does it increase when pace slows to eliminate challenge. Rigor emerges when students are supported to remain engaged with demanding material.

Thus, pacing decisions are not secondary adjustments; they are central to instructional integrity.

The Cost of Misreading Readiness

When educators misinterpret disengagement as willful behavior rather than readiness information, responses often escalate unnecessarily. Common reactions include increased verbal control, repeated directives, or premature task simplification.

Each of these responses carries instructional cost.

- Escalation shifts attention away from content.

- Over-directing reduces cognitive agency.

- Simplification lowers demand rather than adjusting access.

In contrast, posture-driven instruction (Chapter 1) allows educators to pause, reassess, and recalibrate without abandoning learning goals.

Picture Walks, Book Talks, and Instructional Preparation

In early literacy contexts, readiness is intentionally supported through preparatory practices such as picture walks and book talks. These practices are sometimes dismissed as ancillary or expendable under time pressure.

They are not.

Picture walks serve as **cognitive and linguistic scaffolding**, allowing students to preview narrative structure, vocabulary, and thematic content before decoding demands are introduced. Book talks extend this preparation by inviting students to anticipate meaning, ask questions, and establish relevance.

These practices do not dilute rigor. They **preserve it** by reducing unnecessary cognitive load.

As outlined in *Groundwork* (pp. 47–49), preparation is not pre-teaching answers; it is orienting students to engage productively with uncertainty.

Classroom Illustration: Reading Readiness in Practice

A second-grade teacher introduces a new text during a literacy block. The planned objective involves inferential comprehension.

During the picture walk, several students eagerly contribute observations. Others remain quiet. One student fidgets, eyes moving between peers rather than the text.

The teacher notices the uneven engagement and extends the picture walk briefly, asking:
"What do you think might be happening between these two characters?"

She accepts multiple responses without evaluation and transitions into reading.

Midway through the text, comprehension falters. Rather than pressing forward, she pauses:
"I'm noticing this part feels heavier. Let's reread it together."

She maintains the inferential objective but adjusts pace to support access.

The lesson remains rigorous. Engagement is restored.

Adjusting Pace Without Lowering Rigor

Adjusting pace does not require reducing expectations. It requires **changing how time is used**.

Strategies include:

- rereading without simplifying

- pausing for clarification rather than explanation

- inviting multiple interpretations

- allowing silence for processing

These adjustments maintain cognitive demand while increasing accessibility. They reflect the principle articulated in *Groundwork*: structure supports learning when it protects thinking rather than performance (pp. 30–31).

A Necessary Clarification: This Is Not Differentiation by Dilution

Concerns are often raised that responsiveness leads to uneven expectations. This chapter explicitly rejects that framing.

Adjusting pace is not the same as reducing challenge. Nor is it synonymous with individualized curriculum. Instead, it is an acknowledgment that **shared content requires flexible timing**.

Equity is not achieved through identical delivery. It is achieved through shared access to meaningful thinking.

The Educator as Reader of the Room

Reading readiness is an instructional skill. It develops through attentiveness, reflection, and experience. Teachers learn to read rooms not by following scripts, but by observing how instruction is received.

This skill is central to professional expertise. It cannot be automated. It cannot be replaced by pacing guides.

As *Groundwork* emphasizes, professional judgment is not an obstacle to fidelity; it is the mechanism through which instruction remains alive (pp. 33–35).

Why This Chapter Matters

Without attention to readiness, instruction becomes performative. Lessons proceed, objectives are stated, and content is delivered, but learning remains uneven.

This chapter situates pace as a moral and instructional decision, not a logistical one. It asks educators to consider not how quickly they can move, but how long students can stay engaged with thinking.

Chapter Knowledge Check

1. In this chapter, pace is described primarily as:

    - A. A scheduling concern

    - B. A classroom management tool

    - C. An instructional decision affecting access to rigor

    - D. A student-controlled variable

2. Why does the chapter argue that adjusting pace does not lower rigor?

    - A. Because rigor is unrelated to difficulty

- o B. Because pace and expectations are separate
- o C. Because access to thinking preserves demand
- o D. Because assessments compensate for pacing

3. Which practice best supports reading readiness without simplifying content?

- o A. Shortening texts
- o B. Eliminating ambiguity
- o C. Picture walks and rereading
- o D. Reducing inferential questions

Chapter Close

This chapter extends the argument that instruction must respond to human conditions without surrendering intellectual purpose. Readiness is not an obstacle to rigor; it is the gateway through which rigor becomes possible.

The chapters that follow examine how awareness, regulation, language, and task design further support this work.

Instruction does not slow down to accommodate learning. It adjusts so learning can occur.

Practice

Chapter 3

Facilitating Awareness Through Instruction

Attention, Noticing, and the Language That Makes Thinking Visible

Using Academic Tasks to Surface Thought

Awareness is often treated as a prerequisite; students either possess or lack. In practice, it is neither fixed nor internally generated. Awareness is shaped, invited, and sustained through instruction itself.

This chapter advances a central claim: **awareness is not something educators extract from students; it is something instruction produces**. When awareness is absent, it is rarely because students are unwilling or incapable. More often, it is because instruction has failed to orient attention in a way that makes thinking possible.

In *Groundwork*, awareness was positioned as the first condition of learning readiness, preceding regulation, interaction, and reasoning (see *Groundwork v3*, pp. 18–22). This chapter extends that argument by examining how instructional design, particularly within literacy contexts, actively cultivates awareness without diverting attention away from academic content.

Awareness Before Comprehension

Educational discourse frequently assumes comprehension as the starting point of learning. Students are expected to understand directions, content, and purpose before meaningful engagement can occur.

This assumption is flawed.

Awareness precedes comprehension. Before students can understand a text, a task, or a question, they must first be oriented to it. Orientation includes knowing **where to look, what to attend to, and which features matter**. Without this orientation, comprehension becomes accidental rather than supported.

This is particularly evident in early literacy settings, where students encounter texts that exceed their decoding capacity. Yet even in upper grades, students regularly confront dense language, unfamiliar structures, and abstract concepts that require instructional guidance to access.

Awareness, then, is not remedial. It is foundational.

Attention as an Instructional Outcome

Attention is often framed as a behavioral expectation, something students are supposed to give. In reality, attention is an outcome of effective instructional design.

Students attend when:

- the task is intelligible

- the focus is clear

- the demand is appropriately scaffolded

- the environment feels predictable and safe

When these conditions are absent, attention fragments, not as defiance, but as a rational response to cognitive overload or ambiguity.

In *Groundwork* (pp. 26–28), attention was reframed as a relational phenomenon rather than an individual trait. This chapter builds on that reframing by situating attention within the structure of academic tasks themselves.

Picture Walks, Book Talks, and the Architecture of Awareness

Preparatory practices such as picture walks and book talks are sometimes dismissed as preliminary or optional. This chapter asserts the opposite: **they are core instructional moves that establish the conditions for thinking.**

Picture walks invite students to notice visual cues, relational positioning, emotional tone, and narrative progression. They provide a shared reference point before language complexity is introduced.

Book talks extend this work by allowing students to articulate expectations, questions, and hypotheses. These practices do not supply answers. They create **cognitive landmarks** that students can return to during reading.

Importantly, these practices are not limited to early grades. Previewing structure, examining headings, and anticipating argument flow serve similar functions in upper-grade texts.

Awareness is built when instruction makes structure visible.

Language as a Tool for Orienting Thought

The language educators use shapes how students approach tasks. Language can narrow attention prematurely or invite expansive noticing.

Consider the difference between:

- "What is the main idea?"

- "What are you noticing so far?"

The former assumes readiness for abstraction. The latter invites observation without pressure to conclude.

Language that supports awareness:

- emphasizes noticing over correctness

- delays evaluation

- invites multiple perspectives

- signals that thinking is in progress

As articulated in *Groundwork* (pp. 52–54), language frames the cognitive stance students adopt. When language is overly directive, students focus on compliance. When language is invitational, students focus on meaning-making.

Classroom Illustration: Awareness in Practice

In a first-grade classroom, a teacher introduces a picture book during a literacy block.

Before reading, she asks:
"What do you notice about how the characters are standing?"

Students point, gesture, and describe. Some focus on facial expressions. Others notice distance between characters. The teacher does not correct or rank responses.

After reading, she asks:
"Did anyone notice something new after hearing the words?"

Students revise earlier observations. Connections emerge organically between image and text.

No emotional disclosure is requested. No comprehension questions are imposed prematurely. Awareness develops through instruction.

Awareness Is Not a Separate Skill

A critical clarification is required: awareness is not an add-on skill to be taught in isolation. It is embedded within academic work.

Pulling students aside to "work on awareness" removes it from the very contexts where it matters. Instead, instruction should be designed to **surface thinking within content**, allowing awareness to emerge as students engage meaningfully with tasks.

This distinction preserves academic integrity while supporting developmental readiness.

Why This Matters

When awareness is neglected, instruction relies on assumption rather than support. Students are expected to know where to look, how to listen, and what to prioritize without guidance.

This chapter positions awareness as an instructional responsibility rather than a student deficit. It affirms that when instruction orients attention deliberately, students are more likely to engage, persist, and comprehend.

Chapter Knowledge Check

1. According to this chapter, awareness is best described as:

    - A. An internal student trait

- o   B. A prerequisite students must master independently

- o   C. A condition supported through instructional design

- o   D. A behavioral expectation

2. Why are picture walks and book talks considered foundational rather than optional?

- o   A. They reduce the difficulty of texts

- o   B. They replace comprehension instruction

- o   C. They orient attention and structure thinking

- o   D. They manage classroom behavior

3. Which type of instructional language best supports awareness?

- o   A. Language that emphasizes correct answers

- o   B. Language that accelerates abstraction

- o   C. Language that invites noticing without evaluation

- o   D. Language that limits interpretation

Chapter Close

Awareness does not emerge through insistence. It emerges through orientation.

When instruction makes structure visible, language invitational, and tasks intelligible, students learn how to attend, not because they are told to, but because attention becomes possible.

In the chapters that follow, this cultivated awareness becomes the foundation upon which regulation, interaction, and reasoning are built.

Learning does not begin with comprehension.
It begins with noticing.

Practice

Chapter 4

Regulation as Instructional Support

Pausing, Scaffolding, and Task Design Inside the Lesson

What Regulation Looks Like When Learning Is Possible

Regulation is frequently misunderstood in educational contexts. It is often framed as an internal emotional state students are expected to manage independently or as a behavioral condition to be enforced externally. Both framings miss the instructional reality.

Regulation is not a personal achievement students either possess or lack. It is a **context-sensitive condition that emerges, or deteriorates, within instruction itself**.

This chapter advances a critical distinction: regulation is not something teachers demand; it is something instruction supports. When regulation is present, learning is accessible.

When regulation is disrupted, learning becomes fragile, not because students are unwilling, but because conditions no longer support sustained engagement.

In *Groundwork*, regulation was positioned as the second capacity in the learning sequence, following awareness and preceding interaction and reasoning (*Groundwork v3*, pp. 22–27). This chapter examines what regulation looks like inside academic lessons and how educators can restore it through instructional choices rather than emotional intervention.

Regulation Is Visible Before It Is Named

One of the most important insights for educators is that regulation is **observable long before it is verbalized**. Students communicate their regulatory state through posture, facial expression, motor activity, and attentional focus.

Common indicators of regulation include:

- open body posture rather than defensive positioning

- relaxed facial muscles rather than tension or grimacing

- eye focus aligned with task demands

- tolerance for pause, effort, and uncertainty

These indicators are not diagnostic tools. They are **instructional information**.

When educators attend to these signals, they gain real-time feedback about whether learning conditions are intact. Importantly, these signals do not require labeling, calling out, or interpretation aloud. They simply inform instructional decision-making.

Regulation as Readiness, Not Compliance

A persistent error in classroom practice is equating regulation with compliance. Quiet bodies, stillness, and silence are often mistaken for readiness. In reality, these behaviors may mask disengagement, anxiety, or withdrawal.

Regulation is not about control. It is about **capacity**.

A regulated student can:

- remain cognitively present

- tolerate challenge

- persist through effort

- recover from confusion

These capacities matter academically. They determine whether students can engage with complex texts, multi-step problems, and collaborative tasks.

As emphasized in *Groundwork* (pp. 28–30), behavior communicates readiness, not obedience. Regulation must be understood through that same lens.

Instruction Can Restore Regulation

When regulation deteriorates, the most common response is behavioral correction. This approach assumes the problem lies within the student and must be fixed through redirection or consequence.

This chapter proposes a different approach: **adjust the task, not the child**.

Instructional shifts that support regulation include:

- reducing simultaneous demands

- modeling thinking aloud

- providing shared entry points

- pausing to reorient attention

- adjusting pacing without reducing rigor

These moves do not require emotional discussion or disclosure. They restore regulation by making the task more accessible without lowering expectations.

Classroom Illustration: Regulation Inside Instruction

In a fourth-grade math classroom, students are solving a multi-step problem independently. Most sit cross-legged, bodies open, eyes on their work.

One student begins to frown. His arms cross tightly across his chest. His pencil stops moving.

The teacher notices but does not comment on behavior.

Instead, she says to the class:
"Let's work through the first step together before you continue."

She models her thinking aloud on the board, narrating how she approaches the problem.

The student's posture softens. His arms uncross. He resumes work.

No emotional labeling occurs. No correction is issued. Regulation is restored through instruction.

Scaffolding as a Regulatory Tool

Scaffolding is often discussed in terms of cognitive support. It also functions as a regulatory mechanism.

When students are overwhelmed, scaffolding reduces unnecessary cognitive load. When students are disengaged, scaffolding reintroduces structure and purpose.

Effective scaffolding:

- clarifies entry points

- reduces ambiguity without eliminating challenge

- supports persistence

Poor scaffolding, by contrast, either overwhelms students with complexity or removes thinking entirely.

As outlined in *Groundwork* (pp. 46–48), scaffolding works best when it supports thinking rather than replaces it.

Pausing as an Instructional Move

Pausing is frequently misinterpreted as lost time. In reality, pausing is often the moment when regulation is restored.

Strategic pauses allow students to:

- reorient attention

- recover from cognitive overload

- integrate new information

Pauses do not require explanation or apology. They are not admissions of failure. They are **intentional instructional choices** that protect learning conditions.

Why Regulation Does Not Require Emotional Naming

A crucial boundary must be maintained: supporting regulation does not require emotional processing or disclosure.

This chapter deliberately avoids therapeutic framing. Regulation is addressed **through task design, pacing, and instructional stance**, not through emotional interrogation.

This distinction protects both students and teachers. It ensures classrooms remain academic spaces while acknowledging the human conditions under which learning occurs.

Why This Matters

When regulation is misunderstood, teachers feel pressure to manage emotions rather than facilitate learning. Students feel scrutinized rather than supported.

By treating regulation as an instructional condition, educators reclaim their professional role. They respond to what learning requires rather than what behavior demands.

Regulation becomes teachable, not through naming, but through structure.

Chapter 5

Literacy as the Primary Carrier

Reading, Writing, Speaking, and Listening as Practice Spaces

Discussion and Text as Neutral Ground

Literacy occupies a unique position in instructional life. Unlike many academic domains, it requires students to engage simultaneously with language, perspective, structure, and meaning. It asks learners to hold ambiguity, consider alternatives, and revise thinking, all within a shared symbolic space.

This chapter advances a central claim: **literacy is the most reliable instructional carrier for complex human skills precisely because it is not about the self**. Text creates distance. Discussion creates shared reference. Together, they provide a neutral ground where thinking can develop without personal exposure.

In *Groundwork*, literacy was positioned as the connective tissue through which awareness, regulation, and interaction become observable within academic work (*Groundwork v3*, pp. 50–56). This chapter extends that argument by examining how the four ELA domains function as structured practice spaces, containers that hold complexity without requiring emotional disclosure or behavioral management.

The Four Domains as Instructional Containers

Reading, writing, speaking, and listening are often treated as discrete skills. Instructional frameworks divide them for assessment and planning purposes. In practice, however, they function as **interdependent containers** for cognitive and social work.

Each domain offers a different form of access:

- **Reading** allows students to encounter ideas at a controlled pace.

- **Writing** allows students to externalize and organize thinking.

- **Speaking** allows ideas to be tested publicly.

- **Listening** allows students to encounter perspectives without immediate response.

These domains do not merely transmit content. They **hold process**. They give students a place to practice attention, tolerance for uncertainty, reasoning, and revision without centering the self.

This containment is what makes literacy uniquely suited for developmental work inside academic instruction.

Why Stories Carry More Than Information

Stories have long been recognized as vehicles for meaning. What is less often acknowledged is their instructional utility as **protective distance**.

When students engage with characters rather than personal experience, they are able to:

- examine consequences without self-exposure

- consider motivation without confession

- explore conflict without personal risk

This distance is not avoidance. It is a form of safety that allows complexity to surface.

As noted in *Groundwork* (pp. 54–55), narrative allows students to "try on" thinking positions without being required to defend them personally. This is not incidental; it is the reason stories remain such powerful instructional tools across age levels.

Text as Neutral Ground

Neutral ground does not mean value-free. It means **shared reference**.

When discussion is anchored in text, disagreement becomes analytical rather than personal. Students can argue interpretation rather than identity. They can revise thinking without losing face.

This neutrality is critical. Without it, discussion often collapses into opinion trading or moral positioning. With it, discussion becomes reasoning.

The instructional move "Let's go back to the text" is not a redirection away from engagement; it is a redirection toward it. It signals that meaning is negotiated through evidence, not assertion.

Classroom Illustration: Literacy Holding Complexity

In a fifth-grade small group discussion, students debate a character's decision. Voices rise slightly. Perspectives diverge.

Rather than intervening to manage tone or mediate emotion, the teacher says:
"Let's go back to the text."

She asks students to locate the passage that informs their position. The conversation shifts. Students reread. Evidence is cited. Interpretations are refined.

No moral conclusion is imposed. No emotional coaching is offered. The discussion deepens because the text holds the disagreement.

Speaking and Listening as Paired Practices

Speaking and listening are often treated asymmetrically. Speaking is emphasized as participation; listening is treated as compliance.

This chapter rejects that framing.

Listening is not passive. It is an active cognitive practice that requires attention, inhibition, and interpretation. Speaking, when properly structured, requires precision and accountability to shared meaning.

Together, they form a **reciprocal practice space** where ideas circulate and evolve.

As discussed in *Groundwork* (pp. 58–60), discussion becomes productive when students are supported to listen for understanding rather than for response. Literacy-based discussion provides that structure.

Writing as Thinking Made Visible

Writing offers a unique affordance: it slows thinking down.

When students write, they are required to sequence ideas, clarify relationships, and confront gaps in understanding. Writing externalizes cognition, making it available for reflection and revision.

Importantly, writing does not require emotional disclosure to serve this function. Analytical writing, response journals, and explanatory paragraphs all provide opportunities for students to practice organization, reasoning, and precision within academic boundaries.

Why Literacy Protects Rigor

A common concern is that using text as a developmental space dilutes academic rigor. This chapter argues the opposite.

Literacy protects rigor by:

- anchoring discussion in evidence

- requiring precision of language

- sustaining complexity over time

- supporting revision rather than resolution

When literacy is treated as the primary carrier, rigor is preserved not through speed or volume, but through depth and persistence.

Why This Matters

Without a neutral carrier, developmental work becomes either explicit emotional instruction or behavioral management. Both approaches place undue burden on teachers and students.

Literacy offers an alternative. It allows educators to support awareness, regulation, interaction, and reasoning **without naming them**, simply by designing instruction that uses text as shared ground.

This is not incidental to learning. It is central to it.

Chapter Knowledge Check

1. According to this chapter, literacy functions primarily as:

   - A. A content delivery system
   - B. A set of isolated skills
   - C. A structured practice space for complex thinking
   - D. A behavior management tool

2. Why is text described as "neutral ground"?

   - A. It removes values from discussion
   - B. It limits student interpretation
   - C. It provides shared reference without personal exposure
   - D. It prevents disagreement

3. Which instructional move best preserves rigor during disagreement?

   - A. Mediating emotions
   - B. Imposing resolution
   - C. Returning to textual evidence
   - D. Limiting discussion

Chapter Close

Literacy does more than teach students how to read and write. It gives them a place to practice thinking in the presence of others, safely and rigorously.

When instruction uses text as the carrier, complexity is not avoided. It is held.

In the chapters that follow, this shared ground becomes the foundation for task design, questioning, and decision-making.

Skills do not develop in isolation.
They develop where language gives them room to breathe.

Chapter 6

Designing Tasks That Invite Thinking

Ambiguity, Choice, and Productive Struggle

Why Over-Clarity Can Shut Learning Down

Instructional tasks do more than organize activities. They determine what kind of thinking is permitted, who can enter the work, and how learning unfolds once students are inside it.

This chapter advances a central claim: **tasks either invite thinking or replace it**. When tasks are overly prescriptive, thinking narrows. When tasks are vague, thinking disperses. When tasks are intentionally open, structured yet unresolved, thinking becomes necessary.

In *Groundwork*, task design was framed as a structural choice that signals what matters in learning (see *Groundwork v3*, pp. 61–66). This chapter extends that argument by examining how ambiguity, choice, and struggle function instructionally, not as obstacles to learning, but as conditions that make learning possible.

The Misunderstanding of Clarity

Clarity is often treated as an unquestioned good. Teachers are encouraged to make directions explicit, outcomes visible, and expectations precise. While clarity has an important role, its instructional value is frequently overstated.

Clarity supports access when it:

- identifies purpose

- establishes boundaries

- clarifies criteria

Clarity undermines learning when it:

- predetermines thinking

- narrows response options prematurely

- converts reasoning into compliance

The problem is not clarity itself, but **over-clarity**, instruction that answers the question before students have a reason to ask it.

Ambiguity as an Instructional Necessity

Ambiguity is often conflated with confusion. This chapter draws a sharp distinction between the two.

- **Confusion** overwhelms.

- **Ambiguity** invites interpretation.

Well-designed ambiguity signals that meaning is not yet settled and that students are expected to participate in its construction. This expectation is essential for higher-order thinking.

As argued in *Groundwork* (pp. 63–64), learning requires space for uncertainty. When instruction removes that space, students learn to wait for direction rather than engage with possibility.

Open-Ended Does Not Mean Unstructured

A persistent critique of open-ended tasks is that they lack rigor or coherence. This critique misunderstands the nature of instructional openness.

Open-ended tasks are not vague. They are **bounded**.

They:

- establish a shared focus

- invite multiple approaches

- require justification

- resist single correct answers

Structure exists, but it does not dictate conclusions. Students must decide what matters, how to approach the task, and how to support their thinking.

This design preserves rigor while expanding access.

Choice as Cognitive Entry, Not Personal Preference

Choice is often misused in classrooms as a motivational tool, students choose topics, formats, or partners. While these choices may increase engagement, they are not inherently cognitive.

This chapter defines instructional choice differently. Instructional choice invites students to:

- prioritize information

- select evidence

- determine relevance

- justify reasoning

These choices are intellectual, not personal. They require students to weigh options and commit to a line of thinking.

As emphasized in *Groundwork* (pp. 67–68), reasoning develops when students are required to choose among possibilities rather than follow predetermined paths.

Productive Struggle as Evidence of Learning

Struggle is often treated as a problem to be eliminated. In reality, struggle is often the point at which learning becomes visible.

Productive struggle:

- signals engagement with complexity

- indicates cognitive effort

- precedes insight

Unproductive struggle occurs when tasks lack structure or support. Productive struggle occurs when tasks are challenging but accessible.

The distinction lies not in the student, but in the task.

Equity Through Multiple Entry Points

Equity is frequently misunderstood as sameness. This chapter rejects that framing.

Equitable task design provides **multiple entry points into shared intellectual work**. Students may engage at different levels, through different lenses, or with different emphases, yet still participate meaningfully.

Prescriptive tasks, those that specify exact steps, responses, or interpretations, privilege students whose experiences align with the assumed norm. They exclude others not because of ability, but because of misalignment.

Open tasks invite lived experience without requiring disclosure. They allow students to draw on prior knowledge, cultural context, and perspective as intellectual resources.

Classroom Illustration: Writing as Invitation

In a middle school writing class, the teacher introduces a prompt.

Instead of:
"Write three reasons the character made this choice."

The prompt reads:

"What do you think matters most here, and why?"

Students respond differently. Some focus on motivation. Others on consequence. Others on context.

Each response is valid, not because all answers are equal, but because each is **reasoned**.

The task does not tell students what to think. It requires them to decide.

Why Prescriptive Tasks Shut Learning Down

When tasks prescribe:

- how many ideas to generate

- which points to include

- how to structure responses

Students learn that thinking is about fulfilling requirements rather than constructing meaning. Engagement becomes procedural. Curiosity recedes.

This does not make instruction more efficient. It makes it shallower.

Why This Matters

Tasks are the point of contact between curriculum and student thinking. They operationalize instructional values.

When tasks invite thinking, students practice decision-making, persistence, and justification within academic boundaries. When tasks close thinking, students practice compliance.

This chapter positions task design as one of the most powerful levers educators have, not because it controls students, but because it shapes the conditions under which thinking can occur.

Chapter Knowledge Check

1. According to this chapter, over-clarity undermines learning because it:

    - o A. Confuses students

    - o B. Removes necessary structure

    - o C. Predetermines thinking

    - o D. Reduces accountability

2. What distinguishes productive struggle from unproductive struggle?

    - o A. Student motivation

    - o B. Task design and support

    - o C. Time spent

    - o D. Grade level

3. How does open-ended task design support equity?

    - o A. By lowering expectations

    - o B. By allowing identical responses

- ○ C. By providing multiple entry points

- ○ D. By avoiding assessment

Chapter Close

Thinking does not emerge from precision alone. It emerges when students are invited to engage with uncertainty inside structure.

Tasks that leave room for interpretation, choice, and struggle do not weaken instruction. They strengthen it by making thinking unavoidable.

In the chapters ahead, this task design becomes the foundation for questioning, feedback, and instructional response.

Clarity tells students what to do.
Well-designed tasks ask them to think.

Chapter 7

Questioning That Opens, Not Closes

*Coaching Language and Prompts That Support Reasoning
Over Correctness*

Why Questions Shape Thinking More Than Answers

Questions are often treated as neutral instructional tools,
simple checks for understanding or mechanisms for
assessment. In practice, questions are far more
consequential. They signal what counts as thinking, who is
permitted to speak, and how knowledge is constructed within
the classroom.

This chapter advances a central claim: **questions do not
merely reveal thinking; they shape it**. The form, timing, and
posture of a question determine whether students engage in
reasoning or retreat into answer-seeking behavior.

In *Groundwork*, language was identified as a primary
structuring force in instruction, capable of inviting or

constraining engagement (*Groundwork v3*, pp. 52–54). This chapter extends that argument by examining questioning as a form of coaching, language that orients students toward exploration rather than evaluation.

The Hidden Power of Questions

Every question carries an implicit message. Some questions ask students to recall. Others ask them to comply. Still others ask them to risk thinking publicly.

Questions that close learning typically:

- signal that an answer already exists

- reward speed over deliberation

- privilege those already confident

- collapse complexity prematurely

Questions that open learning:

- invite interpretation

- allow partial thinking

- tolerate uncertainty

- require justification

The difference is not subtle. It determines whether students learn to reason or to guess.

Correctness as an Instructional Cul-de-Sac

Single-answer questions are often defended as efficient. They allow teachers to move quickly, verify comprehension, and maintain pace. However, their instructional cost is frequently underestimated.

When questions are framed to produce a single correct response, students quickly learn:

- that thinking is about getting it right

- that risk carries penalty

- that silence is safer than speculation

This framing disproportionately affects students who require more processing time, those developing language proficiency, and those whose reasoning does not align neatly with expected formulations.

Correctness narrows participation. Reasoning expands it.

Coaching Language as Instructional Stance

Coaching language differs from evaluative language in both tone and intent. Its purpose is not to judge responses, but to **extend thinking**.

Coaching questions:

- "What makes you think that?"

- "What are you noticing so far?"

- "Can you say more about that?"

- "How does this connect to what we read earlier?"

These prompts do not supply answers. They signal that thinking is ongoing and that ideas are worth developing.

As noted in *Groundwork* (pp. 69–71), coaching language positions the educator as a facilitator of reasoning rather than an arbiter of correctness. This stance invites sustained engagement.

Developmental Generosity in Questioning

Developmentally appropriate questioning is often misunderstood as simplification. In reality, it is an act of **cognitive generosity**.

Generous questions:

- meet students where they are without lowering expectations

- allow multiple levels of response

- invite participation without embarrassment

This generosity is particularly critical in early grades, where language development and conceptual understanding are still emerging. Asking a second-grade student to identify a "main idea" may be linguistically premature. Asking what "feels important" invites attention without abstraction overload.

The goal is not to avoid rigor, but to sequence it.

Classroom Illustration: Invitation in Practice

In a second-grade classroom, students complete a shared reading. The teacher considers asking:
"What is the main idea of this story?"

Instead, she asks:
"What feels important here?"

Hands rise. Responses vary. One student mentions a character's choice. Another points to a repeated phrase. A third notes how the story ends.

The teacher listens. She asks follow-up questions that deepen reasoning:
"What made that stand out to you?"
"Where do you see that in the text?"

Comprehension emerges through exploration, not extraction.

Why Questions Must Precede Conclusions

When instruction moves too quickly toward conclusion, students are denied the opportunity to wrestle with meaning. Questions that invite exploration create space for uncertainty, a necessary condition for learning.

As argued in *Groundwork* (pp. 72–73), ambiguity is not a failure of instruction. It is evidence that thinking is underway.

Questions should open doors, not close conversations.

Equity Through Invitation

Questioning practices have equity implications. Who is invited to speak, whose ideas are taken up, and how responses are valued shape students' sense of belonging.

Open-ended questions:

- allow diverse entry points

- validate partial thinking

- reduce linguistic barriers

- support participation across confidence levels

When questioning centers on reasoning rather than correctness, classrooms become more inclusive without sacrificing intellectual rigor.

Why This Matters

Questions are among the most frequent instructional moves teachers make. Their cumulative impact is profound.

When questions close thinking, students learn to perform. When questions open thinking, students learn to reason.

This chapter positions questioning not as a technique to be mastered, but as an instructional posture to be cultivated.

Chapter Knowledge Check

1. According to this chapter, questions shape learning primarily by:

- ○ A. Checking comprehension
- ○ B. Maintaining pace
- ○ C. Signaling what kind of thinking is valued
- ○ D. Reducing discussion time

2. Why do single-answer questions often limit engagement?

- ○ A. They are too difficult
- ○ B. They reward speed over reasoning
- ○ C. They reduce teacher control
- ○ D. They increase ambiguity

3. What distinguishes coaching language from evaluative language?

- ○ A. Coaching language avoids feedback
- ○ B. Coaching language delays assessment
- ○ C. Coaching language extends thinking rather than judging it
- ○ D. Coaching language lowers expectations

Chapter Close

Questions are never neutral. They either invite students into thinking or position them outside it.

When educators ask questions that open rather than close, they create classrooms where reasoning is expected, risk is tolerated, and engagement is sustained.

In the chapters that follow, questioning becomes the bridge between task design and feedback, linking student thinking to instructional response.

Answers end conversations.
Good questions begin them.

Practice

Chapter 8

Responding to Error Without Control

Feedback as Information, Not Judgment

Keeping Students Engaged When Things Go Wrong

Error is one of the most revealing moments in instruction. It exposes how students are thinking, where meaning breaks down, and how learning is unfolding in real time. Yet error is also one of the moments most likely to be mishandled.

This chapter advances a central claim: **how educators respond to error determines whether learning continues or collapses**. When error is treated as failure, students disengage. When error is treated as information, students persist.

In *Groundwork*, learning was framed as a developmental process rather than a performance outcome (*Groundwork v3*, pp. 24–26). This chapter extends that framing by examining feedback not as correction, but as instructional response, language and action that either preserve or erode students' willingness to think publicly.

Error as Evidence, Not Deficit

A persistent misconception in education is that errors indicate gaps that must be fixed before learning can proceed. While errors do reveal misunderstanding, they also reveal **engagement**. Students who attempt complex tasks will err. Students who avoid error rarely learn.

Error signals that a student is:

- attempting to apply knowledge

- testing a hypothesis

- navigating uncertainty

These are precisely the conditions under which learning occurs.

As noted in *Groundwork* (pp. 34–36), difficulty is not evidence of incapacity. It is evidence of work in progress. Error must be understood within that frame.

The Language of Feedback Shapes Risk

Feedback is never neutral. The words educators choose communicate whether risk is safe or dangerous.

Judgmental feedback:

- narrows participation

- signals evaluation over exploration

- prioritizes correctness over reasoning

Informational feedback:

- surfaces thinking

- invites revision

- sustains engagement

The difference often lies in subtle linguistic shifts.

Consider:

- "That's not right."

- "That tells me how you're thinking."

The second response reframes error as data rather than deficiency. It keeps the student inside the learning process.

Correction Versus Invitation

Correction seeks to replace an incorrect response with a correct one. Invitation seeks to understand how the response emerged.

This chapter argues that **invitation preserves learning where correction often ends it**.

Invitational responses:

- ask students to explain reasoning

- revisit evidence

- compare approaches

- refine ideas

These responses do not avoid accuracy. They delay it until thinking has had space to develop.

As emphasized in *Groundwork* (pp. 70–71), learning deepens when students are supported to revise rather than instructed to comply.

Classroom Illustration: Error as Entry Point

In a sixth-grade science lab, students label data collected from an experiment. One student mislabels a variable.

The teacher notices and says:
"That tells me what you're thinking. Let's look at it together."

She asks the student to explain the label choice. Together, they examine the data table and the experimental question.

The student revises the label.

There is no embarrassment. No public correction. The class continues engaged.

The error becomes an instructional moment rather than a disciplinary one.

Psychological Safety as an Instructional Condition

Psychological safety is often discussed in organizational contexts. In classrooms, it functions as a prerequisite for effort.

Students will not risk thinking if they anticipate embarrassment, dismissal, or loss of standing. This is not fragility; it is rational behavior.

Instructional environments that treat error as information:

- sustain effort over time

- encourage participation

- support revision

- normalize struggle

As discussed in *Groundwork* (pp. 29–31), safety is not about comfort. It is about predictability, knowing that effort will not be punished.

When Things Go Wrong

Not all errors are small or easily resolved. Some moments involve confusion, frustration, or visible disengagement. The instinct to regain control in these moments is understandable, and often counterproductive.

Control-oriented responses:

- shut down thinking

- shift focus to behavior

- reduce cognitive demand

Instructional responses:

- pause

- reframe

- model

- re-enter the task

The difference is not permissiveness versus rigor. It is **control versus continuation**.

Why Invitation Sustains Engagement

Invitation keeps students oriented toward learning even when outcomes are uncertain. It signals that mistakes are part of the process, not interruptions to it.

This stance does not eliminate standards. It preserves them by keeping students engaged long enough to meet them.

Why This Matters

How educators respond to error accumulates over time. Students learn whether classrooms are places to perform or places to think.

When error is treated as information, classrooms become spaces where risk is tolerated and effort sustained. When error is treated as failure, classrooms become spaces of avoidance.

This chapter positions feedback as one of the most powerful instructional tools available, not because it corrects, but because it communicates what learning means.

Chapter Knowledge Check

1. According to this chapter, error primarily functions as:

     - A. Evidence of misunderstanding

     - B. A signal for correction

     - C. Information about student thinking

     - D. A disruption to instruction

2. Which type of feedback best sustains engagement?

     - A. Immediate correction

     - B. Public evaluation

     - C. Informational, invitational language

     - D. Reduced expectations

3. Why is psychological safety essential for learning?

     - A. It increases comfort

     - B. It prevents struggle

     - C. It supports sustained risk-taking

     - D. It limits accountability

Chapter Close

Error is not the enemy of learning. Avoidance is.

When educators respond to mistakes with curiosity rather than control, they keep students inside the work. Learning continues not because errors are ignored, but because they are understood.

In the chapter that follows, this stance toward error becomes the foundation for decision-making, how students learn to weigh options, anticipate consequences, and choose paths forward.

Mistakes do not interrupt learning.
They reveal it in motion.

Practice

Chapter 9

Decision-Making as Instruction

Academic Choices, Social Choices, and Consequence Awareness

How Reasoning Becomes Visible Through Action

Decision-making is often treated as a life skill, important, but external to academic instruction. In classrooms, it is frequently framed as a behavioral expectation rather than an intellectual process. Students are asked to "make good choices," usually defined as those that align with adult direction or classroom norms.

This chapter rejects that framing.

Decision-making is not an add-on to instruction. It is **one of its most observable outcomes**. When students make decisions, about approach, collaboration, persistence, or interpretation, they reveal how they are reasoning. These moments make thinking visible in ways no worksheet or assessment can.

In *Groundwork*, reasoning was described as the integration of awareness, regulation, interaction, and task engagement (*Groundwork v3*, pp. 73–77). This chapter extends that argument by examining decision-making as the point where those capacities converge and become actionable.

Decision-Making as Reasoning, Not Rule-Following

A critical distinction must be established: decision-making is not synonymous with compliance.

Compliance asks students to follow rules. Decision-making asks students to **evaluate options**, consider context, and anticipate consequences. These are intellectual acts.

When decision-making is reduced to rule-following:

- reasoning is bypassed

- agency is diminished

- learning becomes performative

When decision-making is treated as reasoning:

- students practice evaluation

- consequences become meaningful

- accountability is internalized

As emphasized in *Groundwork* (pp. 74–75), learning deepens when students are supported to think through choices rather than simply adhere to expectations.

Context and Consequence

No decision exists in isolation. Decisions are shaped by context, social dynamics, task demands, time constraints, and prior experience. They also carry consequences, both immediate and long-term.

Instructional decision-making involves helping students notice:

- what factors are influencing their choice

- what options are available

- what outcomes might follow

This noticing does not require moralizing or correction. It requires **making the reasoning process explicit**.

When educators focus on consequence rather than correctness, students learn to think beyond immediate reward or avoidance.

Helpful Versus Hurtful: A Functional Lens

Rather than framing decisions as right or wrong, this chapter introduces a functional lens: **helpful versus hurtful**.

This distinction shifts attention from judgment to impact. It asks students to consider how choices affect:

- the task

- the group

- their own learning

This lens is not permissive. It requires students to weigh consequences and take responsibility for outcomes.

As discussed in *Groundwork* (pp. 76–77), functional framing supports accountability without shame. It keeps students engaged in reflection rather than defensiveness.

Classroom Illustration: Decision-Making in Real Time

During group work, disagreement emerges. Voices rise. Progress stalls.

Instead of intervening to resolve the conflict, the teacher asks:
"What options do you see right now?"

Students pause. One suggests taking turns. Another proposes dividing tasks. A third suggests revisiting the directions.

The teacher asks:
"What might happen if you choose each option?"

Students articulate trade-offs. They decide together.

The conflict becomes an instructional moment. Reasoning is practiced. Consequence awareness develops.

Academic Decisions Are Decision-Making Too

Decision-making is not limited to social situations. Academic work is filled with choices:

- which strategy to use

- when to ask for help

- how to revise writing

- whether to persist or disengage

These decisions often go unnoticed because they occur quietly. Yet they are central to learning.

Instruction that highlights these choices helps students recognize decision-making as part of academic thinking rather than something separate from it.

Why Educators Must Resist Solving

The impulse to solve problems for students is strong, particularly when time is limited. However, solving removes the very thinking instruction aims to cultivate.

When educators step back and ask questions instead of providing solutions, they:

- preserve student agency

- support reasoning

- allow consequences to inform learning

This restraint is not absence. It is facilitation.

Decision-Making as Integration

Decision-making integrates every capacity discussed in this book:

- awareness of internal and external cues

- regulation of impulse and emotion

- interaction with others

- reasoning through options

When these capacities function together, students are better equipped to navigate both academic and social demands.

This integration reflects the coherence of the instructional ecosystem described throughout *Groundwork*, not as a checklist, but as a living system.

Why This Matters

When decision-making is treated instructionally, classrooms shift from control-oriented environments to learning-oriented ones. Students are not managed into compliance; they are supported into competence.

This shift does not eliminate boundaries. It strengthens them by rooting expectations in reasoning rather than authority.

Chapter Knowledge Check

1. According to this chapter, decision-making is best understood as:

    o   A. Rule compliance

    o   B. Behavioral management

    o   C. Reasoning made visible through action

    o   D. Emotional self-control

2. Why is the "helpful versus hurtful" lens instructional?

   - ○ A. It avoids accountability
   - ○ B. It replaces consequences
   - ○ C. It focuses attention on impact rather than judgment
   - ○ D. It simplifies decision-making

3. Why is educator restraint important during decision-making moments?

   - ○ A. It saves time
   - ○ B. It reduces conflict
   - ○ C. It preserves student reasoning and agency
   - ○ D. It limits discussion

Chapter Close

Decision-making is not a detour from learning. It is learning made visible.

When educators treat choices as opportunities for reasoning rather than occasions for control, students develop the capacity to think through complexity, anticipate consequences, and act with intention.

In the final chapter, this integration comes into focus, clarifying the educator's role in facilitating learning without drifting into compliance or therapy.

Thinking does not end with understanding.
It continues through choice.

Practice

Chapter 10

Practice With Boundaries

What Facilitation Is, and What It Is Not

Preventing Drift Into Compliance or Therapy

Every instructional stance carries risk. One risk is rigidity, teaching reduced to compliance and control. The other is drift, instruction that slips into therapeutic or moral territory under the banner of care. Both undermine learning.

This final chapter advances a clarifying claim: **boundaries are not constraints on good teaching; they are what make good teaching possible**. Facilitation without boundaries becomes diffuse. Structure without facilitation becomes punitive. The work of the educator lives in the disciplined space between these extremes.

Throughout *Groundwork*, instruction has been positioned as a human act grounded in awareness, regulation, interaction, and reasoning. This chapter integrates those capacities by defining the educator's role with precision, articulating what facilitation requires and, equally important, what it explicitly does not.

Why Boundaries Matter in Instruction

Boundaries are often misunderstood as barriers to responsiveness. In reality, they function as **containers that protect learning**.

Clear boundaries:

- preserve academic purpose

- protect students from inappropriate exposure

- protect educators from role confusion

- maintain instructional coherence

When boundaries are absent, teachers are implicitly asked to manage emotions, resolve personal narratives, or enforce moral norms, roles for which classrooms are neither designed nor equipped.

As emphasized earlier in *Groundwork* (pp. 79–82), coherence in instruction depends on knowing what belongs inside the classroom and what does not.

Facilitation Defined

Facilitation is an instructional stance, not a personality trait. It is defined by how educators respond to student thinking, behavior, and emotion **through the lens of learning**.

Facilitation is:

- **non-judgmental**: responses do not assign moral value to thinking or behavior

- **non-punitive**: mistakes and disruptions are addressed instructionally, not through consequence

- **developmentally appropriate**: expectations align with students' cognitive and linguistic capacity

- **content-anchored**: discussion and response remain grounded in academic material

Facilitation keeps students inside the work. It does not remove challenge; it supports engagement with it.

What Facilitation Is Not

Just as important as defining facilitation is naming what it is not.

Facilitation is not therapy.
Classrooms are not clinical spaces. Educators do not diagnose, treat, or process emotional experience. Acknowledging emotion is not the same as analyzing it.

Facilitation is not emotional interrogation.
Students are not required to explain feelings, disclose personal experiences, or justify emotional responses. Curiosity is directed toward thinking, not internal states.

Facilitation is not behavior management.
Behavior is addressed insofar as it affects learning

conditions. The goal is not control, but restoration of access to instruction.

Facilitation is not moral correction.
Educators do not position themselves as arbiters of right and wrong. They support reasoning about impact and consequence without imposing value judgments.

These boundaries are not exclusions. They are protections.

Classroom Illustration: Boundaries in Action

During a shared reading, a student becomes visibly emotional. Tears well. The room quiets.

The teacher pauses and says:
"Let's pause here."

She does not ask why. She does not invite explanation. She does not redirect attention to the student.

After a moment, she returns to the text:
"Let's read the next paragraph together."

The student remains included. The class continues. Learning is not derailed, and no one is exposed.

This is facilitation with boundaries.

Preventing Drift Into Compliance

One form of drift pulls instruction toward compliance. In these environments, structure becomes control, questions become tests, and behavior becomes the primary focus.

This drift often occurs under pressure, time constraints, accountability demands, or classroom disruption. The antidote is not permissiveness, but **intentional facilitation**.

Facilitation resists compliance drift by:

- prioritizing reasoning over obedience

- maintaining access to thinking during disruption

- responding instructionally rather than punitively

Boundaries ensure that structure serves learning rather than suppressing it.

Preventing Drift Into Therapy

The opposite drift moves instruction toward therapy. Emotional awareness becomes emotional processing. Discussion becomes disclosure. Teachers are asked to hold material they cannot ethically or practically manage.

This drift often emerges from care without clarity.

Boundaries prevent therapeutic drift by:

- keeping responses content-centered

- acknowledging emotion without probing it

- returning consistently to shared academic material

This protects students from exposure and teachers from role overload.

Why Boundaries Protect Everyone

Boundaries are not about distance. They are about **integrity**.

They protect:

- students' privacy
- teachers' professional role
- the instructional mission of the classroom

When boundaries are clear, students know what to expect. Educators know how to respond. Learning remains the focus.

As *Groundwork* has argued throughout, structure that protects thinking does not inhibit care, it makes care sustainable.

Why This Matters

Without boundaries, educators are pulled in competing directions. They are asked to teach, counsel, manage, and judge simultaneously. This is neither fair nor effective.

By defining facilitation clearly, this chapter returns educators to their professional center: **supporting learning through structure, language, and intentional response**.

Boundaries do not limit teaching.
They allow it to breathe.

Chapter Knowledge Check

1. According to this chapter, boundaries primarily function to:

- A. Limit responsiveness
- B. Enforce compliance
- C. Protect instructional coherence
- D. Reduce emotional expression

2. Which response best reflects facilitation with boundaries?

- A. Asking students to explain their feelings
- B. Ignoring emotional moments
- C. Acknowledging emotion and returning to content
- D. Applying consequences

3. Why is facilitation distinct from therapy?

- A. Therapy lowers expectations
- B. Facilitation avoids emotion
- C. Facilitation remains content-anchored and role-appropriate
- D. Therapy is faster

Chapter Close

This book has argued for instruction that honors how learning actually happens, through awareness, regulation, interaction, reasoning, and choice. None of that work is possible without boundaries.

Boundaries clarify roles. They protect students. They sustain educators. Most importantly, they keep learning central.

Facilitation is not everything.
It is exactly enough.

With this clarity, the work of teaching remains what it has always been: a human act, supported by structure, guided by intention, and grounded in respect for how learning unfolds.

Nothing more is required.

Afterword

What Remains

This book was not written to introduce a new framework, nor to persuade educators to adopt a programmatic identity. Its purpose has been more modest, and more demanding.

It has sought to articulate what many experienced educators already know but are rarely given language to defend: that learning is a human process before it is a systemized one, and that instruction functions best when it aligns with how humans actually engage, regulate, interact, reason, and decide.

Nothing presented here requires educators to abandon their curriculum, standards, or professional judgment. On the contrary, the work assumes that judgment already exists. What it offers is coherence, a way of understanding how daily instructional decisions relate to one another, and how structure can support rather than constrain learning.

If this book has done its work, it has not added complexity. It has clarified it.

What This Book Leaves Behind

This text does not close with a call to action, a checklist, or an implementation plan. Those would contradict its central premise.

Instead, it leaves behind a stance.

A stance that recognizes:

- that readiness is conditional, not moral

- that regulation is visible, not private

- that literacy provides safe distance for complex thinking

- that tasks shape equity

- that questions invite or exclude

- that error is information

- that decision-making reveals reasoning

- and that boundaries protect learning

These are not innovations. They are instructional truths made explicit.

A Note on Professional Trust

Throughout this book, the educator has been positioned as a thinking professional, not a technician, therapist, or enforcer.

This positioning is intentional.

The work of facilitation described here cannot be scripted without losing its integrity. It depends on attentiveness, restraint, and responsiveness, capacities that experienced educators already possess.

This book does not teach those capacities.
It honors them.

Where This Work Lives

The ideas articulated in *Groundwork* are not meant to live on shelves or in professional development binders. They live in moments, often brief, often unnoticed, where an educator chooses how to respond rather than react.

They live in:

- a pause instead of a correction

- a question instead of an answer

- a return to text instead of a moral conclusion

- a boundary held instead of a role expanded

These moments are not dramatic. They are cumulative.

Over time, they shape classrooms where learning is sustained not through control, but through coherence.

Final Word

Teaching does not require more from educators.
It requires clarity about what already matters.

When instruction aligns with how learning unfolds, classrooms do not become easier, but they become truer.

And in that truth, both students and teachers are able to remain present, engaged, and human.

Nothing more is required.

Practice

About the Author

Dr. Lori Ellen Pisani is an educator, coach, and educational leader with more than 35 years of experience supporting children, teachers, and school communities. Known to many simply as *Grauntie*, she has spent her career working at the intersection of learning, emotional readiness, and human development.

Dr. Pisani's work is grounded in a deep belief that education is fundamentally relational; that learning happens best when teachers are supported as people, not treated as parts of a system. Throughout her career, she has been a steady advocate for educators, often described as the leader who stood beside her teachers, protected their dignity, and reminded them of their value when pressure and systems pushed otherwise.

As a coach and mentor, she is recognized for her calm presence, practical wisdom, and ability to help teachers think clearly in complex environments. Rather than prescribing methods or enforcing compliance, Dr. Pisani focuses on posture, readiness, and decision-making; helping educators reconnect with *why* they teach and *how* learning actually becomes possible in real classrooms.

She is the co-creator of the **PKP™ (Pisani–Kershaw Program)**, a literacy-aligned, SEL-grounded instructional framework designed to provide structure without constraining professional judgment. Through *The Grauntie Series*, she speaks directly to educators in a conversational, reflective voice; offering insight, tools, and questions meant to support growth rather than demand perfection.

Dr. Pisani believes teachers deserve clarity, care, and systems that allow good teaching to breathe. Her work continues to center that belief; one conversation, one classroom, and one educator at a time.